The ABCs of Plants

Bobbie Kalman

Crabtree Publishing Company
www.crabtreebooks.com

AaBbCcDdEeFfGgHh

The ABCs of the Natural World

Created by Bobbie Kalman

Dedicated by Katherine Kantor
To Terra Robinson–the smartest, brightest, most creative girl I know.

Author and Editor-in-Chief
Bobbie Kalman

Editors
Reagan Miller
Robin Johnson

Photo research
Crystal Sikkens

Design
Bobbie Kalman
Katherine Kantor
Samantha Crabtree (cover)

Production coordinator
Katherine Kantor

Illustrations
Barbara Bedell: pages 5 (bottom right), 8, 12 (purple flower/right),
    14 (top and middle), 18 (small bees), 19, 24 (bottom left and right), 27
Katherine Kantor: pages 6 (top right and bottom), 18 (butterfly/bottom left)
Bonna Rouse: pages 5 (bottom left), 6 (top left), 12 (red flowers and
    purple flower/left), 14 (bottom), 15, 18 (bee/bottom right),
    24 (top left and right), 25, 26, 28
Margaret Amy Salter: pages 5 (top), 12 (yellow flower),
    18 (all butterflies except bottom left), 21
Tiffany Wybouw: page 18 (wasp/left)

Photographs
© Dreamstime.com: page 6
iStockphoto.com: pages 8, 9 (middle left), 10 (top), 18, 20 (top), 26 (inset),
    27 (except inset), 29 (except letter 'Y')
Jon Sullivan/PD Photo.org: page 19 (inset)
© Shutterstock.com: front cover, back cover, pages 1, 3, 4, 5, 7,
    9 (all except top and middle left), 10 (middle and bottom), 11,
    12, 13, 14, 15, 16, 17, 19 (all except inset), 21 (bottom left), 22, 23,
    26 (except inset), 27 (inset), 28, 29 (letter 'Y'), 30, 31
Other images by Digital Stock and Digital Vision

Library and Archives Canada Cataloguing in Publication

Kalman, Bobbie, 1947-
    The ABCs of plants / Bobbie Kalman.

(The ABCs of the natural world)
Includes index.
ISBN 978-0-7787-3413-0 (bound)
ISBN 978-0-7787-3433-8 (pbk.)

    1. Plants--Juvenile literature. 2. English language--Alphabet--Juvenile
literature. I. Title. II. Series: ABCs of the natural world

QK49.K325 2007   j570   C2007-904238-4

Library of Congress Cataloging-in-Publication Data

Kalman, Bobbie.
    The ABCs of plants / Bobbie Kalman.
        p. cm. -- (The ABCs of the natural world)
    Includes index.
    ISBN-13: 978-0-7787-3413-0 (rlb)
    ISBN-10: 0-7787-3413-7 (rlb)
    ISBN-13: 978-0-7787-3433-8 (pb)
    ISBN-10: 0-7787-3433-1 (pb)
    1. Plants--Juvenile literature. 2. English language--Alphabet--
Juvenile literature. I. Title. II. Series.

QK49.K15 2007
580--dc22

2007026978

Crabtree Publishing Company

www.crabtreebooks.com   1-800-387-7650

Published in Canada
Crabtree Publishing
616 Welland Ave.
St. Catharines, Ontario
L2M 5V6

Published in the United States
Crabtree Publishing
PMB16A
350 Fifth Ave., Suite 3308
New York, NY 10118

Published in the United Kingdom
Crabtree Publishing
White Cross Mills
High Town, Lancaster
LA1 4XS

Published in Australia
Crabtree Publishing
386 Mt. Alexander Rd.
Ascot Vale (Melbourne)
VIC 3032

Contents

About plants

Plants are living things. There are many kinds of plants. Trees and flowers are plants.

Plants make food in their leaves.

Plants live in soil, sand, water, and on rocks. Most plants have **roots**, **stems**, and **leaves**.

Stems hold plants upright.

Roots hold a plant in soil. Roots also take in water. Plants need water to live.

B b B b B b B b B b B b B b B b

Biomes are habitats

Plants live in many places all over the world. The places where plants live are called **biomes**. Biomes are the **habitats**, or homes of plants and other living things. Biomes with many trees and other plants are called **forests**. Forest biomes can be in **tropical**, or hot areas, or in areas with four seasons. Plants also grow in biomes called **wetlands**. In wetlands, many plants grow in water.

Wetlands are areas of land that are under water some or all of the time.

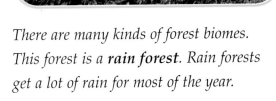

*There are many kinds of forest biomes. This forest is a **rain forest**. Rain forests get a lot of rain for most of the year.*

C c C c C c C c C c C c C c C c

Colorful cactuses

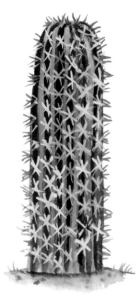

saguaro cactus

Plants called **cactuses** live in **desert** biomes. Deserts are areas that receive very little rain. Cactuses can live without much water. Instead of growing deep, the roots of cactuses grow close to the top of soil. When it rains, the cactuses' shallow roots can **absorb**, or take in, water. Deep roots would miss this water. Cactuses store water inside their thick stems.

barrel cactus

The leaves of this prickly pear cactus look like needles. Prickly leaves help keep water inside the plant and also keep animals from eating it.

D d D d D d D d D d D d D d D d D d D d

Desert plants

Many kinds of plants grow in deserts. When it rains, a desert can be covered with colorful flowers. The flowers grow and make seeds quickly. The flowers soon die, but their seeds are left behind. When a lot of rain falls again, the seeds grow into new plants.

Joshua tree

sage bush

Mexican poppy

This desert is in Africa. Few plants grow here, but there are some colorful flowers.

E e E e E e E e E e E e E e E e E e E e E e

Energy from the sun

You need energy to do everything. You get energy from food.

Every living thing on Earth needs **energy**. Living things use energy to move and grow. They cannot do anything without it. All energy comes from the sun. How do plants get energy? Plants make food from sunlight, water, and **carbon dioxide**, a gas found in air. Using sunlight to make food is called **photosynthesis**. How do people and animals get energy? They eat food. Without plants, there would be no food!

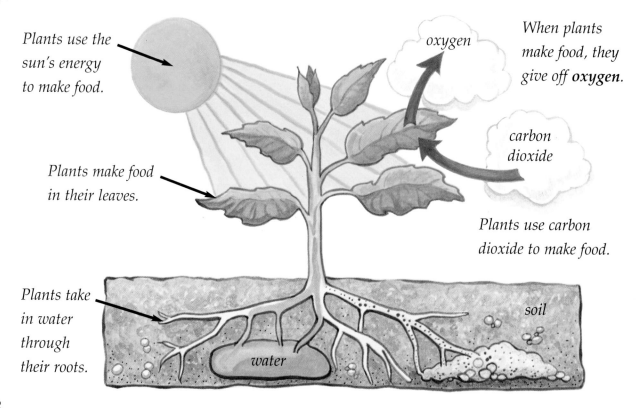

Plants use the sun's energy to make food.

*When plants make food, they give off **oxygen**.*

oxygen

carbon dioxide

Plants make food in their leaves.

Plants use carbon dioxide to make food.

Plants take in water through their roots.

soil

water

 # Food chains

Plants do not use all the food they make. They store some of the food in their roots, stems, leaves, fruits, and seeds. When animals and people eat these plant parts, they get the energy of the sun. The energy is passed along from the plant to another living thing. Passing energy from one living thing to another is called a **food chain**. Follow the food chain shown below.

This child is growing some tomatoes and other plants.

The plants make food using sunlight, carbon dioxide, and water.

Some of the food is stored as energy in different parts of the plants.

These children are using plant foods to make a pizza. When they eat the pizza, they will get the energy of the sun. The energy of the sun is stored in the tomatoes and other vegetables. It will be passed along to the children in a food chain. The children need energy to move, grow, and think.

9

Green power

Most plants have green leaves. Green leaves have **chlorophyll**. Chlorophyll is the **pigment**, or color, which makes the leaves green. Chlorophyll absorbs the sun's energy. The plant uses the sun's energy to change water and carbon dioxide into food. A plant cannot make food without the sun's energy.

In autumn, there is not enough sunlight for plants to make food. The chlorophyll in leaves starts to disappear. The plant cannot make food without chlorophyll. Its leaves fall off. New leaves grow in spring.

H h H h H h H h H h H h H h

Helpful plants

There are many ways that plants help the Earth. Read the list below and then think of other ways plants help our world.

- Plants give us food.

- Plants clean the air. They change carbon dioxide into oxygen. Carbon dioxide is harmful to human beings and animals. We need to breathe oxygen.

- Trees give us shade from the sun.

- Many birds and other animals make their homes in trees. Our homes are made of wood, too. Wood comes from trees.

- Flowers are plants that make our world colorful and beautiful.

(above) Trees give us shade from the sun.

(below) Birds such as owls live in trees.

Imagine!

Many people believe that talking to plants helps plants grow. What would plants say if they could talk to us? Imagine what this plant fairy would tell you and write a story about your conversation with her.

J j J j J j J j J j J j J j J j J j J j J j J j J j

Jack-in-the-pulpit

A Jack-in-the-pulpit can grow to be two feet (63 cm) tall. The plant has a **spathe**, which looks like a hood. It also has a part called a **spadix**, which looks like a tongue hanging out. It is the "Jack" in the **pulpit**. A pulpit is a raised area in a church. This picture shows a pulpit that the flower resembles.

spathe

spadix

pulpit

Kinds of plants

There are many kinds of plants. Trees, grasses, bushes, and flowers are plants. There are other kinds of plants, too. Some plants are shown here.

Flowering plants are the largest group of plants.

Ferns grow in damp, shady places. Ferns can be very big.

Mosses do not have roots or stems. They grow in wet places.

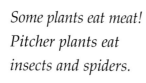

Some plants eat meat! Pitcher plants eat insects and spiders.

14

Life cycle of a flower

A flowering plant starts out as a seed. The seed starts to grow. A stem and small leaves soon form. The plant is now a **seedling**. The seedling has a **bud**. The bud will open into a flower. The flower can soon make new seeds.

seed

seedling

mature flowering plant

bud

15

Meals of Nectar

Animals visit flowers for meals of **nectar**. Nectar is a sweet liquid inside flowers. Bees, butterflies, some birds, and other small animals drink nectar. As they drink nectar, they help flowers make seeds. Do you know how? If you do not know, turn to page 19.

This butterfly is drinking nectar from a flower. Bees use nectar to make honey.

Organic plants

Organic plants are grown naturally. They are grown without **pesticides** or **preservatives**. Pesticides are chemicals that are used to kill the insects that eat plants. Preservatives make foods last longer. Foods with too many chemicals are not good for us. Organic foods are healthier, and they taste better, too!

P p P p P p P p P p P p P p P p P p P p

Pollination

Most plants have flowers. Flowers attract animals with their colors and nectar so that **pollination** can take place. Pollination happens when the pollen from one flower reaches another flower of the same kind. A plant can make seeds only after it has been pollinated. Bees, butterflies, and some birds and bats are **pollinators**. Pollinators carry pollen from plant to plant. Lizards do not drink nectar, but they also pollinate flowers as they look for other pollinators to eat.

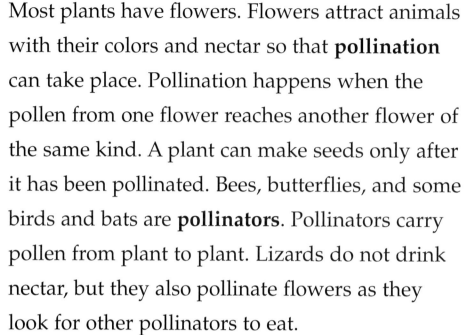

P p P p P p P p P p P p P p P p P p P p

When this bee lands on an apple blossom, some pollen rubs off on its body. The bee then carries the pollen to the next apple blossom it visits and pollinates its flower.

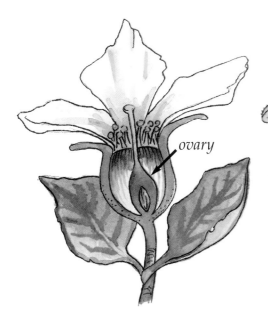

ovary

*The pollinated flower can now make seeds. The **ovary** of the flower will become a fruit.*

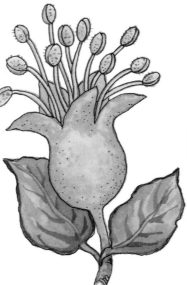

The flower loses its petals. The ovary grows bigger. It will soon be an apple.

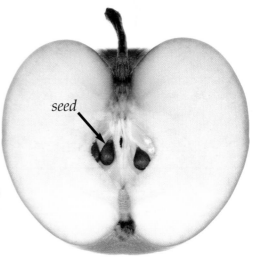

seed

The apple has seeds inside. The seeds will grow into new apple trees.

19

Quiz about plants

Read the whole book before you answer these questions.

1. From where does all energy come? (page 8)
2. Name three parts of plants. (page 4)
3. What do insects do when they visit plants? (pages 18-19)
4. What makes plants green? (page 10)
5. Name a carnivorous plant. (page 26)
6. Name two water plants. (page 27)
7. What do xylem tubes carry? (page 28)

Name two ways that plants help people. (page 11)

R r R r R r R r R r R r R r R r R r R r R r

Rainforest plants

There are more plants and animals in tropical rain forests than in any other biome. Rain forests are hot, and they get a lot of rain, so plants grow year round. Two kinds of plants that grow in tropical rain forests are **bromeliads** and **lianas**.

Bromeliads come in more sizes and colors than any other plants. These plants can grow from the trunks of trees or even on rocks.

Did you know that some plants can climb? Lianas are climbers. They start at the ground and grow upwards toward sunlight. They spread from tree to tree. As they grow, they form bridges, allowing animals to travel between trees. This ape is using lianas to swing from tree to tree.

Seasons of plants

In tropical areas, plants grow all year long. In other places, there are four seasons. The seasons are spring, summer, autumn or fall, and winter. Spring is the start of the growing season for plants. Flowers bloom, and buds form on the trees. Spring is a very colorful time!

In summer, the weather is hot. The leaves of trees are green. Fruit also grows on some trees.

In autumn, the leaves of many trees and plants lose their green color. They turn yellow, orange, and red.

In winter, most trees have lost their leaves, but the leaves of evergreen trees are still green. In winter, there is very little food for animals to eat.

T t T t T t T t T t T t T t T t T t T t

Terrific trees!

conifer tree

Trees are the biggest plants. There are thousands of kinds of trees. Trees have roots, stems, and leaves. The leaves of some trees are like needles. Trees with needle-like leaves are called **conifers**. Conifers have cones. Trees with wide, flat leaves are called **broadleaved trees**. The picture below shows both kinds of trees.

broadleaved tree

Under the ground

The roots of plants grow under the ground or under water. Roots keep plants in place. They also absorb water and **nutrients**. Nutrients help plants, animals, and people stay healthy. We get nutrients from eating food. Plants get nutrients from soil and water.

fibrous roots

adventitious roots

taproot

25

Venus flytrap

Some plants are **carnivores**. Carnivores are living things that eat meat. Venus flytraps are carnivorous plants. Most carnivorous plants live in places where they cannot get enough nutrients from the soil or water. These plants need to get extra nutrients by eating meat. Venus flytraps have **trigger hairs** on their leaves. When an insect or frog touches the hairs, the two sides of the leaf quickly snap shut and trap the animal inside.

trigger hairs

26

W w W w W w W w W w W w W w

Water wonders

Water plants live in ponds, rivers, lakes, and oceans. Their roots, stems, leaves, and flowers are suited to living in water or partly under water. Water plants provide many animals with homes and food. Hyacinths, water lilies, and cattails are three kinds of water plants.

hyacinth

water lilies

cattails

X x X x X x X x X x X x X x X x

Xylem carry water

Xylem is part of a plant. It is a set of tubes that goes from a plant's roots, through its stem, and into its leaves and flowers. The xylem tubes carry water and nutrients from the roots to the rest of the plant.

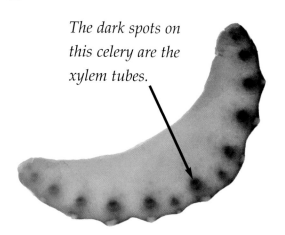

The dark spots on this celery are the xylem tubes.

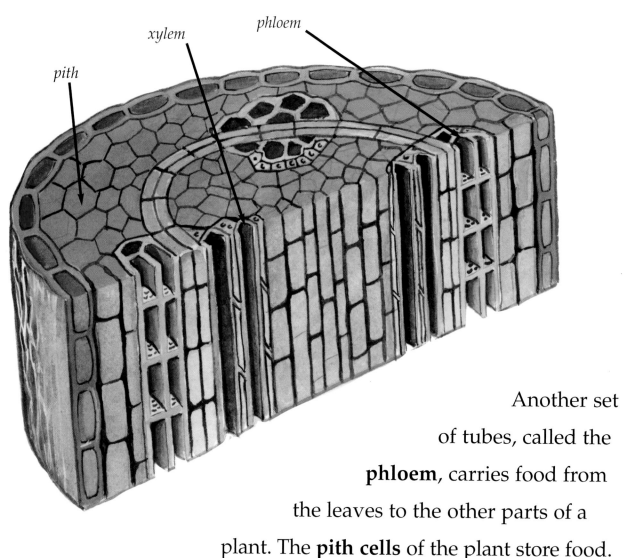

pith

xylem

phloem

Another set of tubes, called the **phloem**, carries food from the leaves to the other parts of a plant. The **pith cells** of the plant store food.

28

Y y Y y Y y Y y Y y Y y Y y Y y Y y Y y Y y Y y

Your plants

Growing plants is fun. When you plant trees, you help clean Earth's air. When you plant vegetables, you give yourself fresh, nutritious foods to eat. When you plant flowers, you help feed insects and other small animals. What will you plant this year?

ZzZzZzZzZzZzZzZzZzZ
Zany plants

Plants can be very weird looking! Take a walk through your neighborhood park and draw pictures of the plants you see.

Do some plants remind you of other things? There are some plants on these pages that look very strange. Which plants look like plants from the time of the dinosaurs? Which looks like an alien?

These trumpet pitcher plants look like they are talking to one another. What would they say about the tree in the picture below them?

AaBbCcDdEeFfGgHh

Glossary

Note: Some boldfaced words are defined where they appear in the book

absorb To take in or soak up

biome A huge area, such as a forest, in which certain kinds of plants grow

carnivore A living thing that eats animals

chlorophyll A green color found in plants that absorbs sunlight in photosynthesis

desert An area of land that gets little rain and where few plants grow

energy The strength needed to move, grow, and change

life cycle The changes in a living thing from the time it comes to life to the time it makes other living things like itself

nutrients Important parts of foods that keep living things healthy

oxygen The part of air that animals and people need to breathe and which plants give off when they make food

seedling A young plant that has grown from a seed

tropical Describing areas that have hot temperatures year round

wetland An area of land that is covered by water for most of the year

Index

Printed in the U.S.A.